THE

CHRISTIAN SOLITARY

GILBERT SHAW

SLG PRESS
Convent of the Incarnation
Fairacres Oxford

2nd Edition (revised) 1971
Fifth Impression 2003

ISBN 0 7283 0046 X
ISSN 0307 1405

ACKNOWLEDGEMENT

Quotations from *The Jerusalem Bible* are by permission of
Darton, Longman &Todd Ltd.

CONTENTS

FOREWORD

More than thirty years after its original publication, I would re-endorse the clear statement of the nature of the Christian solitary life contained in these pages. Such a life bears witness to the very heart of the Gospel of Jesus Christ, and should be undertaken only with that mode of witness in mind. It is an obedience of love, a love tempered by the fire of the Holy Spirit which the Lord desired to kindle on earth. Therefore it needs to be a response to the call of the crucified and glorified Lord to share in his compassion for the suffering world he has come to save. Consequently it is a vocation for those who have already been brought to a spiritual place of stability in their standing before God. They must have come to know that they are sinners, at one with the fallen Adam and Eve, so that by repentance and dependence upon the Holy Spirit they might also stand in the place of re-creation in the union between the second Adam and his Bride, the Church.

In our own day, the true nature of repentance is elusive because thinking, feeling, and even spiritual endeavour begins from the individual, rather from Christ, who has taken our human nature, with its mentality, into himself in God. It is the task of the solitary to restore us, and our whole experience of human creaturehood, to the mind of Christ.

Gregory C.S.W.G.
The Monastery
Crawley Down
Crawley Sussex

Grow strong in the Lord, with the strength of his power. Put God's armour on so as to be able to resist the devil's tactics. For it is not against human enemies that we have to struggle, but against the Sovereignties and the Powers who originate the darkness in this world, the spiritual army of evil in the heavens. That is why you must rely on God's armour or you will not be able to put up any resistance when the worst happens or have enough resources to hold your ground. (Ephesians 6: 10-13, *J.B.*)

In the midst of the conflict described by St. Paul, the created universe depends on man's free response to the divine purpose for 'the whole creation is eagerly waiting for God to reveal his sons'. (Romans 8: 19, *J.B.*) Here is the Christian hope: victory is assured through the divine love revealed in the humanity of the incarnate Son. 'Since God did not spare his own son, but gave him up to benefit us all, we may be certain after such a gift, that he will not refuse anything he can give.' (Romans 8: 32, *J.B.*)

All who are in Christ, baptised by faith into his re-creation are called into the knowledge of and participation in the continuing redemptive work of Christ. By grace we are made members of his kingdom which both is, and is awaiting fulfilment. The solitary vocation is a particular aspect of this call to redemptive unity by, with and in Christ.

There is nothing intrinsically superior in the pattern of life of the solitary to that of the Christian in the world. To think otherwise would be to introduce a double standard, for all Christian vocations must be directed to the perfecting of charity.

All Christians enter into the gift of life and grace but the solitary is called more especially to know the loneliness and cost of the return to holiness. A self-chosen life of solitude, even for more prayer, would lead to disaster because the solitary life must be undertaken in response to a call from God and not as a matter of self-will. It was the complete obedience of the life that Christ offered in love for man's restoration that glorified the Father. So with the Christian solitary it is the life lived that is sacrificial though it is the character of the prayer that enables the life to be thus lived and offered in union with Christ's offering. There can be no redemption without the shedding of blood. There must be death to the natural that it may be transfigured into the spiritual.

> Now this is only to be found in purity of heart. For to know neither envy nor conceit nor anger; never to act out of frivolity; not to seek our own interests; not to take account of evil and all the rest; what is this but continually to offer to God a perfect and pure heart, and to guard it intact from any movement of passion. Purity of heart is then the unique end of our actions and all our desires. It is again this, that we should embrace solitude … to keep our heart invulnerable to all wicked passions and to mount, as by so many degrees, even to the perfection of charity. (Cassian, *First Conference*, VI and VII.)

There is nothing to be gained by self-loss for its own sake. The emptiness of self must be filled with the knowledge of God, above all with the knowledge that he imparts through scripture and the practice of diligent and penitent prayer.

Dispositions and the necessity for training

The experience of the desert Fathers showed that the solitary life, except in the case of a very special call from God, was fraught with danger unless there was sufficient preparatory training in the common life of the coenobium. The Abbot Isaias, an emigrant from Scetis to Palestine, taught that the common life with its ascetic conflict of self discipline may be likened to the bearing of Christ's sufferings and his cross in the way of humble discipleship and the entering into the hermit's cell of quiet to 'the mounting of Christ's cross'. 'If the mind desires to mount the cross before the senses have ceased from their sickness, the wrath of God comes upon it because it has entered upon a measure beyond its capacity.'

Obedience

The first preparation is through obedience in the common life. It is necessary in order to secure balance and control in the individual life so that everything flows from obedience. This is one of the reasons why the solitary way must nearly always develop out of the coenobitic since the spirit is freed principally through purification in the common life. The solitary will only keep his balance in the midst of the demand of the conflict in the 'desert' if his will is absolutely freed, strengthened and purified by obedience.

Obedience to the Spirit is the aim of the solitary. That cannot be known simply by his own idea of what obedience should be but must be formed through consultation and obedience to others, to the tradition and the spiritual Father and Mother. No one can live in the desert without obedience. This obedience is the greatest discipline, but one must look beyond the discipline to the liberty which is the end for which the obedience is established. It is necessary to submit to obedience in order to arrive at liberty.

3

Penitence

If the first disposition is obedience, a necessary corollary is penitence in the realisation of one's own sinfulness. Archimandrite Sophrony is insistent that one must not look on the solitary life as a more perfect way than any other. He once said that on Mount Athos the attitude of the cenobitic to the solitary was that the solitary was very much the servant of everybody on the occasions when he returned to the monastery, and that he was a solitary because he knew he was a great sinner.

The true solitary realises his need of deeper solitude for repentance, both for his own sins and for the whole range of cosmic sin, but this penitence for and understanding of sin arises out of the thirst and desire for God and therefore the solitary must realise that he will be called upon to deepen and develop the process of self-knowledge and of complete abandonment of himself to the will of God which, if he is a professed religious, he should have begun to learn in the coenobitic life. He must also realise that his life is given to God for the Church and in the Church as is that of any professed Religious, and that far from contracting out to satisfy any personal attraction to prayer and silence, he is being drawn further into the conflict of reconciliation.

THE CONFLICT

In the first stage of the conflict in the coenobium the rough edges of his character are rubbed off and the Religious begins to learn simplicity and humility, to walk very humbly before God. In this first stage the Devil attacks him through the weakness of his nature, through his own unconscious levels and in his relationships with other people, stirring up disharmonies and petty jealousies.

When this stage is well worked out, those called to greater solitude will realise they need silence, for only in silence can man wait upon God: 'Be still and know ...' Then may come what can be called 'the poltergeist stage'. The solitary, having attained a certain degree of stability, and having begun to know what silence is and to be alone, may be assaulted on the spiritual level, in some cases by phantasmagoria. St Antony of the desert is an example. Those who reach inner peace are a trouble to the Devil, so if a truly recollected person is put down in an evil place there is bound to be an explosion.

Here is the importance not only of the solitaries but of the contemplatives in community and of the contemplatives in the world. They are bound to be the centre of a vortex because they are not liked by evil. They radiate peace out of a still centre and anything that is against peace will be focussed against them. If their recollection is true, the evil will 'bounce off'. If it does not, it must be met in patient endurance, in chastity and purity of intention, and the power of God will overcome.

The conflict for the solitary will be to preserve and to complete peace in the self and peace beyond the self. There will still be assaults on the integrity of his response to the call to unification, assaults from all that is as yet unreconciled in his own unconscious as well as from the pressures of the world and from demonic influences.

The solitary should set himself the task of opening himself to the gifts of the Spirit, to be permeated by them, through his continual desire for the fruition of Christ's work in him. It is for him to pray continually with the psalmist, 'O turn away mine eyes lest they behold vanity', that is to say: Draw my attention to God and his works so that I am not drawn to or involved in the things which pass away. Make me alive in your way to see all things and to live all things for you.

God gives the gifts but the solitary must open himself to receive them and practise to acquire them. There must be intelligent perception and the desire that will embrace what is perceived and 'trigger off' the will to possess and to be possessed by God.

The desired *apatheia*, the 'passionlessness' of the solitary is directed against all that disturbs or conflicts with the desire that is directed to God, to the acquisition of his gifts and to his will. St. Paul tells us to 'be ambitious for the best, the most excellent gifts'. Covetousness or ambition can destroy man if they are desires for self-expression or self-glorification, but if the natural desires described by these words are converted and re-directed by the Spirit, then they become the very measure of our dependence on and unity with God.

The solitary must make every effort to attain the gifts, but it would be useless to desire them without giving the self to love what it desires and opening the self to assimilate the gifts through self examination and acknowledgment of failure in renewed penitence and dependence.

It is through the perfection of his re-direction of life in order to acquire true sonship that the solitary is made a peace-maker and can himself stand inviolate as a true icon of Christ's victory in the conflict with evil.

Coinherence

Withdrawal does not deprive the solitary of his humanity and all that that implies in terms of relationship, for his coinherence in mankind is his by natural birth. His call by God to a life of withdrawal only alters the way of his association with others. He is still man's servant because he is God's servant, and he looks to the end when all will be complete in an acknowledgement of and dependence on God.

For him solitude is the *milieu* for his growth in a mature relationship with God and in the knowledge of God's will for the world. For him withdrawal emphasises the fact of his relationship with man, because through the deepening of his prayer in solitude he comes to a deeper realisation of his coinherence in mankind.

Reconciliation

His function in the world is that of a mediator who desires that all men should be drawn to respond to God's mercy, to acknowledge and accept the reconciliation accomplished by, with and in Christ. His solitude and silence enable him to become conscious of the world's needs and to go out in love and service to humanity as a whole, rather than to be conscious of detailed needs, except in so far as these are specifically brought to his knowledge.

The cutting off of physical contacts and imaginative stimulation through withdrawal is intended to discipline and purify his apprehension so that the needs and sufferings of the world and of individuals may be appreciated from the standpoint of simple dependence on God. The world and the individual both need God's mercy, and their suffering and distress come from their failure to recognise their need of conversion. The solitary, from his standpoint of simple dependence, is to perceive this truth in his spirit and to give himself to be a channel of the divine mercy for the world. As the natural creative energies of his life are transfigured by the recreative energies of the Spirit, the discord, rebellion and falling short of the natural world are held by his prayer to the judgment and healing of Christ's redeeming love.

The call of the solitary is not to inactivity but to an intensity of activity in the willing offering of the whole self—body, thought, emotion and will—to be purified and unified by obedience to Christ's transforming purpose, that it may grow into the simplicity of the new man in Christ and be wholly given to the ministry of reconciliation in the recreative power of God's love.

Unity

Solitaries realise their relationship with the world both in the conscious and unconscious levels of their soul in the unity of the Spirit. This transcends outward relationship with persons, though for some it will be manifested in outward relationships with people who come to them for counsel as well as those whom they meet of necessity in daily life.

For those called and proved, the solitary way is one of withdrawal from outside interests to wait exclusively on God. It is a separation for God by sacrifice so that the life lived in solitude may bear fruit in the eternal order. It is not a flight from reality but a life which through withdrawal is restored to man's true end: to know God and to know all creation—all men, all time, all space—in God and for the glory of God. The solitary is called to the most total commitment of the self that is possible apart from physical martyrdom for the faith. He is called to be alone with God so that his natural life may be wholly set on God.

We know that at the moment of death there will be nothing but God and the self. Death, man's last enemy, separates man from all physical contact with the world he leaves, and in the grave his body decays. At the moment of death there is nowhere in the natural order where man can hide. He meets the judgment and mercy of God, and in the light of the Spirit of Truth nothing can remain hidden or unacknowledged.

By reason of his vocation the solitary must each day recall the meaning of his separation which is to face the divine mercy in the piercing light of the Spirit that he may learn to live as one dying to the world from which God has called him.

The fruits of life will be harvested at the moment of death, but the life of spiritual sonship is to be lived as fully as possible day by day, for the solitary's whole being, body, soul and spirit, is to be more completely renewed by his life of withdrawal than it could otherwise have been for him. The solitary is called by God to this particular way of renewal, of transformation from the natural life to the new life in Christ, through the testing demands of the life. The vital question for the solitary is, therefore: 'What use do I make of my aloneness with God?'

As the solitary antedates death in his life, so also he antedates the final consummation, for each day his life is directed to that end. In prayer the conflicts and sufferings of the present time are recognised and reconciled in the prayer of Christ. When this truth is fully grasped, there should be a spontaneity of life for the solitary, a joy that flows from the realisation that all things are being renewed in the life-giving Spirit.

The whole life of the solitary should be conformed to the dependence on and openness to God which is prayer. The rule of the solitary, therefore, must be such as will preserve the essential character of his aloneness and provide for that aloneness to be filled with matter for recollection, dependence, penitence and an increasing knowledge of God.

Each solitary will have his own individual rhythm of prayer and offering throughout the twenty-four hours, a rhythm which is the expression of his flexibility and dependence on the Holy Spirit. This is a sphere where he needs to have and to show all possible humility and obedience to the spiritual Father or Mother in order that he does not become self-expressive.

There must be an appropriate rhythm of prayer, Bible study, intellectual study, manual work and physical exercise. To achieve a balanced life some time should be given to handwork and to outdoor work.

The emphasis in the personal prayer of the solitary must be on penitence together with a complete dependence on God in the confidence that he alone can cleanse and perfect the soul's offering and bring to light the individual deformities which hold back or inhibit the complete acceptance of the divine will. In proportion to the measure of self-loss and the increasing overcoming of the risings of self, further grace will be given to endure the conflict with evil which is involved in holding to God's love the world from which the solitary has outwardly retired that he may be sanctified for others through his own complete offering to the will of God. If this is seen as the purpose of the continuing self-loss then the importance of the positive use of the faculties in learning and being occupied in the things of God should be obvious.

Purity of heart and recollection

To achieve this end the immediate aim of the solitary should be purity of heart. In the words of the Abbot Moses:

> Whatever then can help to guide us to this object; viz. purity of heart, we must follow with all our might, but whatever hinders us from it, we must shun as a dangerous and hurtful thing ... We shall always direct our actions and thoughts straight towards the attainment of it for, if it be not constantly fixed before our eyes, it will not only make all our toils vain and useless and force them to be endured to no purpose, and without reward, but it will also excite all kinds of thoughts opposed to one another. For the mind, which has no fixed point to which to return and on which it may chiefly fasten is sure to roam about from hour to hour and minute to minute in all sorts of wandering thoughts, and from those things which come to it from outside to be constantly changed into that state which first offers itself to it. (Cassian, The Abbot Moses, *First Conference.*)

The Abbot Moses here points out the importance of recollection, that is, the gathering together of the self to be directed to the one end for which the self was created, and re-created in Christ, relationship to God and through God to the whole cosmos.

Recollection must be clearly distinguished from concentration which is an intellectual activity by which one thinks hard about one subject and thereby blots out other subjects. Recollection implies the redirection or gathering together of the perceptions in attentive, unstrained waiting upon God. In recollection the individual prepares, in so far as is possible, to receive the gift of contemplation. Here is the importance both of inner silence, the stillness from much thinking, and of solitude that preserves and guards silence.

Intercession

In his more complete withdrawal the solitary should be given to prayer for the unity of all men. In it there should be a minimum of personal effort and a maximum of dependency on God.

There is an intensity of intercessory energy in his separation and solitude which is a necessary service and inspiration to the life of the Church. He should have some specific knowledge about the needs of the Church, the world and human problems so that his intercession may be informed and he may pray with understanding, for as we said above, the solitary is one with all mankind. This knowledge must not be a matter of curiosity but of deep concern. The contemplative life always has had an element of prophecy within it, for the contemplative sees the whole tangle of man's life in its long term aspect as being under the judgment of God, rather than concerning himself with a number of immediate problems leading to particular action.

The solitary must embrace the sufferings, deformities and problems of the world as a whole, because as he realises sin as a whole, he holds all to the mercy of God, for God alone can deal with it and bring good out of the evil. As the solitary comes to fuller union in himself and is participant, as much as God wills, in the desolation that is the knowledge of the separation from God which is caused by the ghastliness of sin, his faith must endure even though hope is so darkened that there seems no hope and only love remains, that with our Lord he may surrender his spirit into the Father's hands. That is when the spirit is being tested in a knowledge that only the spirit can bear. Then, after the darkness, comes the twilight of expectancy before the dawn of full union.

Before there can be any light of contemplation in wisdom there must be elements of dereliction in order that the vision may be apprehended spiritually in and through the Holy Spirit's light, without any desire for personal security, consolation or enlightenment: nothing for the self except that God's will may be done.

In the higher levels of prayer there is an altogetherness, a being caught up and held, a being taken into the stability of true unitive prayer, an awareness of active participation in being unified. The perfecting of the will so as to be completely one with the will of God in Christ takes us into the making up of the fulness of Christ's passion and brings us to the reign of the kingdom of Love in its growing fulfilment on earth. This is the source and end of all true joy.

It is only prayer through the risen, crucified Lord that conquers the world, restores the Church and makes Saints of God's people.

Prayer in its essence is giving our will to be one with the will of God, and the cost is Calvary. The answer to evil is the bringing of the triumph of Calvary into the whole cosmos.

Here and now, in the formation of personality, we give Christ to each other or wound Christ in each other. The heavenly unity, the life in Christ, is the pulse of love, the giving and receiving love, the life of personality.

The whole of this life is ours that there should be such a giving of self that there is nothing in us to hide the face of Love.

We need never be afraid. the unconquerable will cannot be touched so long as it is one with God, and God knows how much we can bear.

We are in the growing life of the infirmity of Love.

The life of sanctification goes through the whole of time and covers the whole of space. It goes into the unity which is heavenly, the eternity which alone can be fully responsive to God.

Death is not an end: it is continuity, the gathering up of all we have done and are and will be. We take with us that which we have learnt in this life, for here and now God has given us Christ that we might live Christ.

In relation to eternity it is not temporal survival that ensures blessedness but obedience. The temporal is blessed through the number of those, through the increase of those, who live for God, who live in Christ's obedience that Christ's reign may be established.

It is the souls wholly given to God who stand firm in the spiritual conflict, standing that the Holy Spirit may do his work. This can only be as we are empty of self, depending on God in simplicity, recognising our sinfulness, knowing we can do nothing of ourselves but only as God works in us.

If the way is hard it is only that the surrender may be more complete. It is the solitary who most completely answers the terror and roughness of the way, for when and where it is hard he looks to the end, and it is for this that the silence and solitude are ordered for God.

The contemplatives are the servants of the Church as the Church is the servant of the world. To them, as to the Church, is given the word of reconciliation and the ministry of reconciliation. The Church bears witness by Word and Sacrament, the contemplatives in prayer and living.

Nothing but contemplation reverses the evil which is at the centre of the spiritual warfare in the confusion of this age of martyrdom which is calling to a martyrdom of blood or of total confessorship. We must be committed to that, to the straight course of answering God's love with our love.

The contemplative is the transmitter of the passion of the Lord.

It is in the understanding of the depths of the passion that the priest and the contemplative are most completely at one because both are called to the heart of the conflict that God's victory may be manifest.

The higher we are lifted in the pillar of the passion, the more we will see, know and he penitent for the deformity of evil, and the more we will be active in the realisation of the divine compassion. We are in the battle, yet there is a place of settled peace, a peace not as the world gives, a peace beyond comprehension, a peace won by Christ's resurrection.

The spirit must be purified that there may be nothing of self but all of God. The end is that the whole of our self which we give to God becomes one living flame of fire, his fire. Therefore be a still flame for God.

For the solitary more than for any other there must be total dependence on God. In this vocation there is the final testing of the spirit, leading on to as complete a union with God as a soul can sustain in this life.

Peace in the heart: nothing left but the love of God

Only in the pouring out of self can we be clothed with the garment of light.

The deep mystery of God is darkness and is beyond all knowledge except the wonder that God is God. Yet we know him in his action, in his love poured out to us, in his desire that all should be saved. We know him in the activity of the sacramental life by, with and in our Lord in the light of the Holy Spirit.

Let us therefore give ourselves to God that he may accomplish his will which is the participation of the creature in the loving action of the Creator.

It is from purity of heart that God's love is mediated in the activity of the Holy Spirit. The fulness of prayer is an entering into the spiritual sphere.

Surely our life is nothing but our union with the whole mystery of Trinity in and through Jesus Christ.